# Preach
# at Large

Collected by

## murray watts

MONARCH
BOOKS

Mill Hill, London NW7 3SA and Grand Rapids, Michigan 49501

Copyright © Murray Watts 2001
The right of Murray Watts to be identified as author of this work has been asserted by him in accordance
with the Copyright, Designs and Patents Act 1988.

First published by Monarch Books in the UK 1999. This edition 2001.
Concorde House, Grenville Place, Mill Hill, London NW7 3SA.
Published in the USA by Monarch Books 2001.

Distributed by:
UK: STL, PO Box 300, Kingstown Broadway, Carlisle, Cumbria CA3 0QS;
USA: Kregel Publications, PO Box 2607, Grand Rapids, Michigan 49501.

ISBN 1 85424 510 4 (UK)
ISBN 0 8254 5997 4 (USA)

British Library Cataloguing Data
A catalogue record for this book is available from the British Library.

Cartoons by Darren Harvey Regan

Designed and produced for the publishers by
Gazelle Creative Productions,
Concorde House, Grenville Place, Mill Hill, London NW7 3SA.
Printed in Singapore.

A curate had suffered a very difficult working relationship with his minister over the three years of his first curacy.
At last, it was time for him to leave.
No more would he have to endure the stubbornness and pedantry
of this impossible man.
He preached his final sermon to the congregation on the text, 'Abide ye here with the ass, and I will go yonder.'

A visiting preacher was aware that he had overstepped the mark with his 45-minute sermon.

'I'm so sorry,' he explained to the verger, 'but there wasn't a clock in front of me.'

To which the verger replied:

'No, but there was a calendar behind you.'

I remember David Watson preaching
on the intimacy of prayer.
He illustrated this by pointing to the reredos
in St Michael-le-Belfrey Church, York,
where the Lord's Prayer is written in full.
The sign-writer had difficulty
getting each phrase onto a separate line,
so the Lord's Prayer begins
- beautifully and simply -
'Our Father which art in heaven, hallo.'

*C H Spurgeon once asked a student for the ministry to preach an impromptu sermon. The result merits an entry in the Guinness Book of Records for the shortest sermon ever. Appropriately, it was on the subject of Zacchaeus, and this is how it went:*

'First, Zacchaeus was a man of very small stature; so am I. Second, Zacchaeus was very much up a tree; so am I. Third, Zacchaeus made haste and came down; so will I.' With that, the student sat down to shouts of 'More, more!' from his fellows.
'No,' said Spurgeon, 'he could not improve upon that if he tried.'

Parishioners arrived at their local church for Morning Worship to discover the doors locked and bolted.
There was a note from the minister:
'You have been coming here long enough. Now go and do it.'

# A PREACHER WAS NOTORIOUSLY BORING.

One Sunday, the verger tried a little experiment to liven up the sermon - he laced the vicar's water with gin. The sermon that followed was remarkable. It was funny, down to earth, full of neat illustrations, hard-hitting and spiritually enlightening. The parishioners were astonished and the verger was jubilant.

The next Sunday, he stepped up the gin in the water and another sensational sermon followed, even more powerful than the first.

On the third Sunday, the bishop was visiting the church so, in honour of this occasion, the verger put nine-tenths gin to one-tenth water. The vicar excelled himself preaching on the story of Daniel in the Lion's Den. The pulpit shook as he paced up and down. He acted the parts, he laughed, he cried, he shouted, he whispered, he touched the hearts of his congregation, he fired their enthusiasm, he inspired them to follow Daniel's example. After the service, the bishop shook the vicar's hand warmly.

'A very good sermon,' he told him, 'but there's only one small point. God sent an angel to shut the mouths of the lions, Daniel didn't "zap them between the eyes and strew their brains across the walls like spaghetti".'

**M**embers of the Elim church were getting carried away in worship. The tambourines were going, the drums were banging, the choruses were flowing in an everlasting stream and the prayers mounted to heaven like a thousand arrows loosed from the quiver. Amidst the sighs and

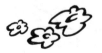

shouts of joy, one old man was overcome with emotion.

'Oh dear Lord!' he called out. 'Thou canst see we're having a blessed time here tonight, Lord, but this is nothing, Lord. Thou shouldst have been at the meeting last Sunday, Lord!'

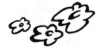

George Whitfield, the great eighteenth-century
preacher, told a story about the most famous
actor of his day, David Garrick.
A preacher asked him,
'How is it that you actors are able, on the stage,
to produce so great an effect with fiction; whilst
we preachers in the pulpit, obtain such small
result with the facts?'
Garrick replied, 'I suppose it is because we
present fiction as though it were fact,
whilst you, too often,
offer facts as though they were fiction.'

Someone had stolen the preacher's bike.
He felt sure that one of his church members
was the thief, so he decided to preach a
sermon on the Ten Commandments.
When he came to 'Thou shalt not steal',
he made a great deal of the commandment,
preaching eloquently about the scourge of theft
and the collapse of standards in our society, but
when he came to the commandment
'Thou shalt not commit adultery,'
he suddenly remembered
where he'd left his bike.

Many years ago a woman was at a mission meeting led by the preacher Gipsy Smith. She wrote to him afterwards:

'Dear Sir, I feel that God is calling me to preach the Gospel. The trouble is, I have twelve children, What shall I do?'

Gipsy Smith replied: 'Dear Madam, I am delighted to hear that God has called you to preach the Gospel. I am even more delighted to hear that he has provided you with a congregation.'

A pastor fell out with his church.
After bitter arguments,
he was forced to leave
and took up a job
as a prison chaplain.
He preached his last sermon
at the church on John 14:1.
'I go to prepare a place for you.'

Church member to minister:

'You'll never know what your
sermon meant to me.
It was like water
to a drowning man.'

*A YOUNG CURATE, TRYING TO WAKE up his sleepy congregation, suddenly interrupted his sermon with the words, 'I remember the time when I was in the arms of another man's wife!' Everyone sat up. 'She was the wife of my father,' he added, to chuckles from the congregation.*

The bishop heard of this incident and decided that the joke would make an excellent introduction to his next sermon. He stood up in the cathedral, before a vast congregation of Lord Mayor, town councillors and civic dignitaries.

'I remember the time when I was in the arms of another man's wife,' he began, with great aplomb. Then there was a long pause. The bishop stammered, 'Just for the moment, I can't remember whose wife she was!'

A bishop tells how he visited a church
and talked to a man who had been
a churchwarden for forty years.
'You must have seen some changes in the
church during your forty years.'
'Yes, I have,' replied the churchwarden,
'and I have opposed every single one of
them!'

A lady asked the Reverend Charles Simeon
if a Christian should always be talking
about religion.
'No, no,' exclaimed the great preacher.
'Let your speech be seasoned with salt -
*seasoned* with salt, madam, not a whole
mouthful!'

Preacher to congregation:

'My job is to preach
and your job is to listen.
If you finish your job
before I've finished mine,
please keep quiet.'

THE LOCAL PRIEST WAS DRIVING down a country lane in his Morris Minor when a Mercedes careered round the bend, spun out of control and crashed into the Morris. Both cars landed in the ditch. The driver of the Mercedes staggered over to the priest.

'By all the saints in heaven!' said the priest, 'you nearly killed me!'

'I'm sorry, Father,' apologised the man, taking a flask of whisky from his pocket. 'Here, have a drink of this, it'll calm your nerves.'

'Why there's more than an ounce of goodness in you, my son,' said the priest, taking a generous swig, 'to be sure, a drop of the old stuff won't go amiss at a time like this.' He took another gulp. 'Here,' he handed the flask back, 'have a swig yourself.'

'Oh, no, Father,' said the man calmly. 'I'll just wait here till the police arrive.'

A new man arrived at the vicarage and was met by the teenage son.

'I'm sorry, my father's busy at the moment - he's just had a phone call offering him an industrial chaplaincy.'

'But he has only been here two years.'

'I know. But he'd get a new car, a big house and a huge salary.'

'What's he going to do?'

'Don't know. He's in the study praying for guidance.'

'And your mother?'

'Oh, she's upstairs packing.'

27

**Mother:** Son, it's getting late. You must get up and go to church!

**Son:** I don't want to go to church.

**Mother:** Give me two good reasons why you shouldn't go to church.

**Son:** First, I don't like the people. Second, the people don't like me.

**Mother:** I don't care. It's getting late, now get up and go to church!

**Son:** Give me two good reasons why I should go.

**Mother:** First, you are 50 years old, and second, you are the minister.

Some preachers
who don't know what
to do with their hands
should try clamping them
over their mouths.

A black church in the ghetto was so poor that the preacher sent round his hat for the offering. When it came back, it was empty. There was a pause. 'Thank you, my children,' said the preacher, 'for sending back the hat.'

*There is a church in Huthwaite, Nottinghamshire, which has a letter missing from a sign outside - it reads: Assemblies of od.' This might describe the people involved in the following incident:*

Many years ago, a wise pastor I knew was approached by a young man who was convinced he was possessed by the Spirit of Cream Buns. Incredible though it sounds, the belief was genuine. He just couldn't stop eating cream buns and was convinced that this was a demonic craving. The pastor did not conduct an exorcism.
(How would one go about such a thing?
Oh Cream Cake come forth!

*cont'd.*

Depart from him, thou Chocolate Éclair!)
My friend, a remarkable man of God, had a
divinely inspired solution. He told the young man
that his problem needed very special treatment. He
should bend over and touch his toes. He did so. Then
the pastor kicked him up the backside and said,
'That's for being such an idiot.'

*This reminds me of my favourite lyric in a gospel song,*
*which has the line:*

'Drop kick me, Jesus, through the goalposts of life!'
This sheds an entirely new light
on the idea of being 'instantly converted'.

A CLERGYMAN WAS SITTING on a bench in Trafalgar Square, eating his lunch, when a man in a grubby raincoat came up to him.

'Naughty postcards, Vicar?'

'Kindly go away,' said the clergyman. The man looked round shiftily, then whispered, 'Naughty but nice, Vicar, eh, lovely postcards, bit of what yer fancy-'

'My dear man,' spluttered the clergyman, 'please leave me in peace to eat my lunch.'

But the man was not to be put off. 'Oh, go on, Vicar, naughty postcards, under the counter, bit of all right, eh, eh, very cheeky postcards, Vicar.'

'Oh, very well,' the clergyman sighed angrily, taking a bundle out of his pocket. 'How many do you want?'

I can still remember the Latin grace that I had to recite at college - but not what it meant. I sympathise with the panic-stricken vicar, who faced with *'Dominus vobiscum'* from his bishop, murmured the reply, *'Er... et tu, Brute!'*

Jonathan Swift surveyed his unpromising congregation and began his sermon. 'There are three kinds of pride - of birth, of riches, and of talents. I shall not speak of the latter, none of you being liable to that abominable vice.'

*One of the sermon illustrations I remember most vividly from my childhood was about a soldier whose life was saved by the Bible in his breast pocket. A bullet went straight into the Bible, getting no further than about the Minor Prophets - which is a great deal further than many people get. However, the bullet failed to reach its destination and the man was saved. The moral was clear: the Word of God is a defence against the enemy and an instrument of salvation.*

*This analogy worked perfectly well until, many years later, I stayed with a lady in the north of Scotland.* *cont'd.*

*She had on her mantelpiece a photo of her Uncle Willie, in First World War uniform, and next to it a copy of his bloodstained New Testament. It had been grazed by a bullet, which had cut a channel through the edge of the pages into his heart. This, I thought, is the penalty of reading only the New Testament.*

*Conversely, what if the British army had all been supplied with Matthew Henry's commentaries? The Germans would have retreated in confusion...*

EVERY DAY, AT PRECISELY 10.32 AM, the local vicar would leave whatever he was doing and go into his study - from where he could see the Inter-City 125 rush past the bottom of his garden.

In the middle of a prayer-meeting, or a planning committee, even during a counselling session, the vicar would get up at 10.32, go into the study and gaze at the express train as it flashed past. One day, the new curate decided to rebuke him gently: 'Isn't your hobby getting a little out of hand?'

'Oh, I'm not interested in train-spotting,' explained the vicar. 'I just like to see the only thing that moves in the parish without my having to push it.'

Two churchwardens were comparing the sermons of the vicar and the curate.
'I prefer the curate, myself,' said the first.
'Why's that?'
'Well, he says "In conclusion" and concludes, and the vicar says "Lastly" and lasts.'

A leaflet passed around a theological college in Salisbury suggested the brilliantly original scheme of 'Chain Vicars'. It read:

*'If you are unhappy with your vicar, simply have your churchwarden send a copy of this letter to six other churches who are also tired of their vicar. Then bundle up your vicar and send him to the church at the top of the list in the letter. Within a week you will receive 435 vicars and one of them should be all right. Have faith in this chain letter and do not break the chain. One church did and got their old vicar back.'*

43

*Lord Soper was famous for his street preaching. On one occasion a heckler sneered at him:*

*'What's it like being a professional Christian?'*

*Lord Soper replied: 'Very much the same as being an amateur, except I don't make so much money.'*

A METHODIST MINISTER WAS WALKING down the street when a very well-dressed man ran up to him and shook him by the hand.

'Reverend,' said the man. 'I'll never forget that brilliant sermon on temperance you preached five years ago. How you told us of the poor working man, spending his wages in the pub with his children dressed in rags, while the publican was driving round in a Jaguar with his family in fur coats and dressed in the height of fashion!'

The minister nodded solemnly. 'And did my sermon reform your life?'

'Oh, it did, it did,' said the man, 'transformed it beyond recognition! I decided to become a publican myself.'

A mother was convinced that her wayward
son would become a Christian.
She lost no opportunity in telling him
that one day he would come to the faith.
She pleaded with him to mend his ways,
to see the light; she sent him little cards
with Bible verses on, spiritual books,
tapes of powerful sermons, all to no avail.
One day, she fell on her knees and prayed
fervently that God would totally remove
the obstacle to her son's conversion.
There was a blinding flash and she vanished.

A woman grudgingly dropped a coin into the collection plate, then sat down to listen to the sermon. Afterwards, she complained loudly at the low standard of the preaching.

Her seven-year-old son interrupted: 'Well, what can you expect for 5p, Mum?'

On the Sunday following the Watchnight Service, the minister gave this notice: 'And would the congregation kindly remember that the box marked "For The Sick" is for financial contributions only.'

Two nuns were driving through the countryside when they ran out of fuel.

They walked to a nearby farmhouse for help and the kindly farmer said that they could siphon some of the fuel from his tractor.

However, they could not find anything in which to carry the fuel, until the farmer produced a battered old chamber pot. The nuns filled the pot with fuel, walked back to the car and began pouring it in. A passing motorist, hardly believing what he saw, stopped and said,

'I don't agree with your religion, but I admire your faith.'

*Billy Graham was walking along the road when an acquaintance pointed out a drunk and observed cynically:*
*'There goes one of your converts.'*
*'He might be one of mine,' replied Billy Graham, 'but he's certainly not one of God's.'*

A long time ago, a parson thought it polite to wait for the country squire before beginning the service in his village church.

One Sunday, he forgot and began with the opening scripture:
'When the wicked man-'
'Stop!' shouted the churchwarden. 'He hasn't come yet.'

*Preacher:* Can everyone hear me at the back?

*Voice from the back:* Yes, but I wouldn't mind changing seats with someone who can't.

'Mummy, do all fairy-tales begin:
"Once upon a time"?'
'No, darling, some of them begin:
"When I became a Christian
all my problems were over."'

# The Latest Decalogue

Thou shalt have one God only; who
Would be at the expense of two?
No graven images may be
Worshipped, except for the currency;
Swear not at all; for, for thy curse
Thine enemy is none the worse:
At church on Sunday to attend
Will serve to keep the world thy friend;
Honour thy parents; that is, all
From whom advancement may befall:

Thou shalt not kill; but need'st not strive
Officiously to keep alive:
Do not adultery commit;
Advantage rarely comes of it:
Thou shalt not steal, an empty feat,
When it's so lucrative to cheat:
Bear not false witness; let the lie
Have time on its own wings to fly:
Thou shalt not covet, but tradition
Approves all forms of Competition.

A WOMAN HAD A DOG which was wildly out of control. No matter how many Good Doggy Training Schools, Perfect Pup Evening Classes or Respectable Rover Correspondence classes she tried, the dog was unmanageable.

One day, a famous Christian healer came to town. She went to his meeting and was deeply impressed. If legs could be lengthened, arthritic joints healed, incurable diseases vanquished, why not a dog trained? She went to the healer and begged him to pray for her dog.

'Leave the dog with me during this mission,' he said, 'and the animal will be spiritually transformed.'

A week later she came back, and sure enough, a miracle had occurred. When the preacher said, 'Come,' instead of running off and digging up the neighbour's flower beds, the dog came; when he said 'Sit' instead of doing a backflip through the french windows, the dog sat; and when he said 'Fetch', instead of collapsing on the ground in a coma, the dog ran after the stick and brought it right back to the feet of the preacher.

'Thank you, thank you,' said the woman, tears of joy in her eyes - but then a worrying thought crossed her mind.

'What if my dog only responds to your voice?'

'Give him a command,' said the preacher, 'anything. I promise you, he'll obey every word!'

'Heel!' she shouted, and the dog sat bold upright, raised its paw in the air and barked:

'Rise up in the name of the Lord!'

THE CHRISTIAN LIFE OF SOME CHURCHGOERS is so inconspicuous that you'd think Christ commanded his followers to 'Go into all the world, shut up and keep your heads down.'

*This approach to life is perfectly illustrated by a police recruit's response to a problem set in a training exam. It read as follows:*

*You are on the beat and you see two dogs fighting. The dogs knock a baby out of its pram, causing a car to swerve off the road, smashing into a grocer's shop. A pedestrian is seriously injured, but during the confusion a woman's bag is snatched, a crowd of onlookers chase after the thief and, in the huge build-up of traffic, the ambulance is blocked from the victim of the crash.*

*State, in order of priority, your course of action.*

He replied: 'Take off uniform and mingle with crowd.'

It is regrettable that many preachers do not take the sound advice about their sermons which is closer than they think - namely, the word: 'Pulp-it'.

An African preacher, speaking on the text, 'What shall it profit a man if he gain the whole world and lose his own soul?', argued that people can lose their souls by being *too charitable*.
His congregation were astonished,
but he went on to explain:
'Many people attend church, hear the sermon and, as soon as the service is over, divide it among their fellows, this part for that man, and that verse for that woman, and such and such a warning for Mr X, and this particular challenge for Mrs X - on and on they go. In this way, they give away the whole sermon and keep none for themselves.'

A certain curate, preaching on
a time to his parishioners, said
that our Lord with five loaves
had fed five hundred persons.
The clerk, hearing him fail,
said softly in his ear:
'Sir, ye err, the gospel is five
thousand.'
'Hold thy peace, fool,' said the
curate. 'they will scarcely
believe that they were five
hundred.'

A Scot was a-preaching how
that all men are one another's
neighbour and brother in
Christ:
'Even the Turk, the Jew, the
Moor, the cannibal, the far
Indian' and then concluded:
'Yea, and the very Englishman
is our neighbour too.'

*(Sixteenth century)*

*One could attempt a useful definition of the art of the preacher, by adapting some words of W H Auden:*

*A preacher is 'someone who talks in someone else's sleep'.*

THE LITTLE CHURCH WAS PACKED to hear the new minister. He was a young man, fresh from theological college, and he climbed up into the pulpit, head high, proud to be giving his first sermon.

He began to deliver his stirring message, but gradually he realised that he was losing the attention of his congregation. Some fell asleep, others stared blankly, one or two got up and left.

By the end of the sermon he felt utterly humiliated and crept down from the pulpit a broken man.

Afterwards, a wise old man - one of the elders of the church - shook his head.

'My boy,' he said gently, 'if only you'd gone up into that pulpit as you came down, you'd have come down as you'd gone up.'

What's the difference between an audience and a congregation? *An audience listens.*

A travelling preacher took his wife to one of his appointments. She was left on her own in the church and eventually sat down in a back pew. A steward came and chatted to her, not knowing who she was but warmly welcomed her to the service.

Afterwards, as she was on her way out, the steward whispered to her confidentially: 'Let me tell you, we don't get a duffer like this in the pulpit every Sunday.'

A MINISTER WAS SPEAKING in the chapel of a psychiatric hospital. In the middle of his sermon, one of his patients stood up and shouted: 'How long have we got to listen to this appalling rubbish?'

The minister turned to the consultant psychiatrist next to him and whispered nervously, 'Shall I stop speaking?'

'No, no, go ahead,' said the psychiatrist.

'But what if he interrupts again?' said the minister, not wanting to cause a scene.

'He won't, I assure you,' said the psychiatrist. 'That man has only one lucid moment every seven years.'

The great nineteenth-century preacher, C.H. Spurgeon, conducted a 'masterclass' on sermons for his students. This was his advice:

**'When you speak of Heaven,
let your face light up,
let it be irradiated by a heavenly gleam,
let your eyes shine with reflected glory.
But when you speak of Hell -
your ordinary face will do.'**

I've heard of a school in rural England which teaches children 'Christian Education' in a very literal sense. If you walk in, you'll see on the walls posters illustrating the numbers one to ten. Not 'one cat,' 'two fishes,' 'three birds' and 'four cows'; but 'one Lord', 'two fishes', 'three days before the Resurrection', 'four gospels, 'five loaves', and so on.

Somewhere is the implication that ordinary things are not holy enough. 'All right, dogs, cats, cows and pigs, off you go! You're not spiritual enough. No grunting, unless it's in Hebrew, and no woofing unless it's theologically correct.'

But if you think this kind of 'Christian Education' is narrow, it's nothing to a little book in my possession which glories in the title: My Jesus Pocket Book of Nursery Rhymes. Unsuitable traditional rhymes have been adapted for the Christian child. For example:

Jack and Jill went up the hill
To fetch some living water
Drank it down and saw they'd found
Joy and life ever after.

*Or there's this one:*

Wee Willie Winkie
Runs through the town,
Upstairs and downstairs
In his nightgown,
Peeping in the window,
What does he see?
The children don't have time for Jesus
They're watching TV.

*Arguably, TV is a great deal more interesting than censored nursery rhymes which don't scan. However there's no limit to the re-writing of our culture. Here's one of mine:*

> Humpty Dumpty sat on a wall,
> Humpty Dumpty had a great fall,
> This gave him the feeling
> To seek Inner Healing
> And now he's no problems at all.

*In fact, if you take this 'Christianising' principle to its logical conclusion, you can't go into a sweetshop with your children to buy ordinary sweets - you have to buy special Christian sweets for them:*

> 'A quarter of Liquorice Allsouls please,
> and a packet of Evanjelly Tots.'

*Or what about,*

> 'Milky Pray: the sweet you can eat during evensong.'

*An unrepentant parishioner*
*accosted the vicar:*
*'Everything you say to me goes in one ear*
*and comes out the other.'*
*'Of course,' smiled the vicar, 'there's*
*nothing in between to stop it.'*

Cleaning out the pulpit, a caretaker found the typescript of the previous Sunday's sermon.

He was intrigued to see that the preacher had pencilled notes to himself in the margin: 'Pause here for effect,' then further down, 'Wipe brow, sigh,' and half-way down the next page, 'Lift hands up to heaven.'

After this there was a long, very involved piece of the sermon which the caretaker couldn't understand at all. Against this the preacher had written: 'Argument woolly and confused. Theology weak. Shout loudly and thump pulpit.'

*A divinity lecturer was speaking at a famous university. On the stroke of twelve, students rudely began to snap their files shut and leave.*

*'Wait, ladies and gentlemen! Wait, please!' said the elderly professor commandingly.*

*'I still have a few more pearls to cast!'*

THE VICAR STEPPED INTO THE PULPIT and opened up the Bible in front of him with a flourish.

'What does that mean, Daddy?' said the little boy in the front row.

'It means that he's going to tell us important things about the Bible.'

Then the vicar took out a sheaf of notes and laid them carefully on the lectern.

'What does that mean, Daddy?'

'That means he's going to explain all the things in the Bible story.'

Then the vicar took off his watch and put it on the side of the pulpit.

'What does that mean, Daddy?'

'That means absolutely nothing at all.'

*Strange how, when some people talk of gifts of the Spirit, they prefer the dramatic ones. They tell of receiving the gift of prophecy, of healing or of speaking in tongues but never, somehow, the gift of administration. Not surprising, really. It doesn't sound very impressive to say:*

*'I was praying fervently the other night and, do you know, suddenly, amazingly, I started to type these letters!'*

*I am told the following incident occurred a few years ago in an English house-church. I cannot verify it but, in some corners of God's Kingdom, fact is usually more bizarre than fiction.*

A small group were praying for a young man. They had gathered round in a circle, laid hands on him, and were desperately hoping that the Holy Spirit would fall on him and that the young man would duly speak in tongues.

Perhaps he was resisting God.

Perhaps there was some unconfessed sin.

Perhaps they all lacked faith - because nothing happened whatsoever. Still speaking English, the young man made his apologies and left, grateful to escape what felt more like a prayer beating than a prayer meeting. The zealous Christians prayed on fervently, convinced that he would soon start speaking in tongues, perhaps on his way home.

Meanwhile, the young man had discovered to his horror that his precious motorcycle had been stolen. Crying, stumbling, he rushed back into the prayer meeting and blurted incoherently:

'S-ss-someone'sstolenmy Kawasaki!'

At which all those in the prayer meeting shouted, 'Praise the Lord! Hallelujah!'

*A story is told of Dr Mahaffy, former provost of Trinity College, Dublin.*
*When asked by a local clergyman how he had liked his sermon, Dr Mahaffy replied:*
*'It was like the peace and mercy of God.'*
*The clergyman was deeply flattered and wanted to know why he was making such a sublime comparison.*
*'Well,' said Dr Mahaffy, 'it was like the peace of God because it passed all understanding, and like his mercy because it showed every sign of enduring for ever.'*

One of the greatest advantages of religious broadcasting is that you can turn it off. Unfortunately, the average pulpit does not have a switch on its side. I sometimes fantasize about having a remote control device for making boring preachers vanish, or a button for fast-forwarding a repetitive train of thought: 'And so, dearly beloved brethren, I come to my main three points again, firstly thesplggffghwheeeeezzzrrr and so, in conclusion, let us say the grace together.'

Bishop Sydney Smith devised the worst
punishment imaginable.
'Sir,' he said to his adversary,
'you deserve to be preached to death
by wild curates.'

*Intercession is desperately needed if the spiritual life of one former MP is anything to go by. The Right Honourable John Ward composed this prayer in 1727:*

'O Lord, thou knowest that I have nine houses in the City of London, and that I have lately purchased an estate in Essex. I beseech thee to preserve the two counties of Middlesex and Essex from fires and earthquakes. And, as I also have a mortgage in Hertfordshire, I beg thee also to have an eye on that county, and for the rest of the counties thou mayest deal with them as thou art pleased.'

*The story is told of Mark Twain attending a service for a charity in New York. Before the sermon, he placed a twenty-dollar bill on the pew ledge. After ten minutes had elapsed, he replaced it with a ten-dollar bill. After twenty minutes, he removed the ten-dollar bill. The preacher droned on for a long time. Finally, when the collection plate came round, Mark Twain took out a twenty-dollar bill.*

**Husband to wife,
overheard in New York subway:
'Honey, if God had wanted
us to have money,
he would have made us
TV evangelists.'**

*A Scottish visitor to the Holy Land was outraged at the cost of a boat trip on the Lake of Galilee.*

*He was told it would be the equivalent of £35.*

*'Do you realise', he exclaimed, 'I can hire a boat for a week on Loch Lomond for that?'*

*'Ah, but sir,' the guide explained, 'these are the waters on which our Lord himself walked.'*

*'No wonder he walked,' said the Scotsman.*

The offering had been taken in the
tiny country church, but at the end of the
service there was a special collection for
missionary work. Most of the parishioners
were poor but they gave generously. Finally,
the bag came round to the lady of the manor.
She turned away haughtily.
'I do not give money to missions.'
'Then take some money out of the bag,
your ladyship,' said the verger,
'this money is for the heathen.'

A curate preaching to his parishioners of the Day of Judgement said:

'At that day Christ will say to me,
"Curate, what hast thou done with my sheep?"
I shall answer:
"Beasts thou gavest them to me and so I
return them to thee."'

(Eighteenth century)

An incident in a Brazilian football match graphically illustrated the point that while there is a time to be on our knees, there is also a time for action. International footballer Roberto Rivelino received the ball straight from the kick-off and drove a shot from the half-way line: the ball whizzed past the goalkeeper's ear while he was still on his knees in the goal mouth completing his pre-match devotions.